You're Full of It!

FAITH

That Is!

Al Furey

PUBLISHING

Manassas, Virginia

ISBN: 978-0-9795489-2-5

Published by Making Life Better Publishing
11404 Balls Ford Road, Manassas, VA 20109
www.mlbpublishing.com

Design and Layout by Fluid Motion

Impreso en Colombia - Printed in Colombia

CONTENTS

PREFACE

Growing up as a teenager in the church in New Zealand, it really bothered me when preachers would come around and say, "Let's all release our faith." I used to sit there and wonder, "How?" It was somewhat of a trend in Spirit-filled churches and after a while I questioned myself. I wondered, "Why can't I release my faith? Do I even have any faith?"

In pursuit of God's revelation on faith, I began to study the topic and discovered some wonderful things along the way. This book is the fruit of this pursuit and years of questioning and study.

I have also come to know that the topic of faith can be highly controversial. So here's your challenge: Even if you don't agree with everything being said about faith, try and look for the Truth. Pursue faith and hunt it down until you have unveiled the essence of it. Then live accordingly.

Meanwhile, here's what I have discovered.

Sincerely,
Al Furey

INTRODUCTION

Years ago I was preaching in Canada. After one of my day sessions I went back to the hotel dejected. I felt my sermon on faith didn't produce anything or help anyone. I cried out to God and said, "When great men of God preach on faith, great things happen. People are often taken into a new realm in God. When I preach on faith, nothing happens. Not only that, but by the time I've finished the message, no one knows what I was talking about. And the truth is, neither do I."

Then the Lord said something I have never forgotten. He said, "You are trying to make it a theological philosophy. When I ministered faith, even the children understood. Faith is simple; it is not a list of do's and don'ts. It is revelation that comes from my Word. When you receive the revelation great things will happen. You are trying to convince them of a truth in a philosophical way when they really need revelation, by my Spirit, in my Word.

You Really Are Full of It

"To every believer is given
the measure of faith."
Romans 12:3 (KJV)

Chapter One
WHAT IS FAITH?

In Hebrews 11:1, the Bible offers us a definition of faith. It says, "Now faith is the substance of things hoped for, the evidence of things not seen."

When we release our faith, it opens the door for God to meet our need. Hebrews 11, also known as the faith chapter, shows that some of the most significant achievements in the Old Testament were the direct result of faith in action. In the same way, the New Testament often indicates that a lack of faith, rather than ability, kept Jesus and his disciples from performing miracles. Jesus kept it simple. In Mark 5:35 (KJV) He said to the ruler of the synagogue whose daughter lay dying: "Be not afraid, only believe." This would have been the same as: Have faith.

I believe we have to be committed to what we believe in order to see results, because everything God has promised in His Word is property we can claim for ourselves.

"Faith is the Substance"
The word "substance" means that which under-

lies, or the foundation for another thing to stand on. If faith is the substance of things hoped for, it means it underlies or is the foundation for everything we hope for. Everything we receive from God rests on the foundation of faith. In the same way a house needs a foundation, we need a foundation of faith on which we can stand and receive God's miraculous and supernatural provision.

In the Greek, the root word for "substance" is the word "underwriting." In other words, faith is the underwriting that guarantees our hopes and desires.

Years ago, I saw a very vivid illustration of what this means when I was still selling insurance. I had sold a policy to a married couple. They filled out the application, signed it and gave me a check for the first month's premium. After I left their home, I drove back to the office only to find a message on my answering machine from the wife. My first instinct was that they had changed their minds and wanted to cancel the policy. I soon learned, however, that after I had left their home that day, the husband drove to a nearby store and was killed in a car accident. Our company paid out the life insurance to the amount of several hundred thousand dollars.

We never deposited the premium. Included in the policy was a clause that said we underwrote to pay out all the money if one of them died. In a similar way, faith underwrites that God will come through for us. Faith is the substance and our insurance. Faith is the certainty of the outcome and a confirmation in our hearts.

"Faith is the Evidence of Things Not Seen"
The word "evidence" is also translated as "title deed." This can mean the checking, clinching agreement. Jeremiah spoke of the "title deed" as the evidence. A title deed is the proof that you own a house.

Jesus often said, "He that believeth hath." You may not always have seen the evidence of answered prayers, but faith is your evidence. Faith comes into being and is activated through the Word of God, which is the seed. (Luke 8:11, NKJ) As we hold on to His promises, we will see the evidence—the fruit of the seed.

Chapter Two
OTHER DEFINITIONS

Over the years I have come across many different definitions and descriptions of faith. Here are some of them:

1. Faith is just trusting God and asking no questions.

This is definitely easier said than done!

"Faith operates regardless of feeling."

2. Faith is what is left over when all the feelings are gone.

Most of us are governed by what we feel. But when faith is in operation, it is immaterial how we feel.

3. Faith is believing that God will do what He says in His Word He will do.

Most of us are very good at explaining away even

God's Word to fit our circumstances. Faith is not passive; faith is not dead. Remember the woman with the issue of blood? (See Mark 5:25-35) This lady, troubled all those years by an issue of blood, said: "If I can touch the hem of Jesus' garment, I shall be made whole." She'd never been around Jesus, she'd never seen Jesus, but she heard He was coming that way. She'd also heard the stories of the miracles. She had to disobey ceremonial law that prohibited her from being on the street, except to go to (what we now call) the doctor. She violated the law to get to Jesus. She went on the offensive - she wasn't passive. She took action. She touched the hem of His garment.

In spite of the crowd, she found a way to touch Him. The Bible says He was actually moving away and she barely got the hem of His garment. Jesus stopped and asked, "Who touched me?" The disciples responded: "Everyone is touching you. They're all around you." But Jesus said, "No, somebody touched me."

Out of all the people, bumping against Him and touching Him, only one touch made Him stop. It was the touch of a little lady. The difference was that her touch had an attitude of believing. She was going after something and she went out and did it.

When Jesus asked who had touched Him, she knew what He was talking about. She knew. And so she responded, "It was me, it was my touch."

"Faith is in active pursuit."

I imagine some of the other people in the crowd said, "Hey, we touched Him too." But she knew. She knew her mission had been accomplished. And Jesus said, "Go your way, your faith has made you whole."

In the Greek that word "faith" literally meant, "your faithfulness to what you did, is what made you whole."

At the outset, she said touching the hem of Jesus' garment would be enough to make her whole. In spite of all the obstacles, she proved faithful and was healed.

"Faith is faithful."

Her faith was active, not passive. She didn't wait for Jesus to come to her; she went to Him, pursuing her healing. She demonstrated one of the great keys to faith with her faithfulness.

4. Faith is trusting the truthfulness of someone else's statements.

When we trust the truthfulness of God's statements, we simply take God at His Word. True faith moves the hand of God. God has never asked us to manifest faith for something He hasn't already promised. You are not trying to get something, you are simply trying to receive what He has already given.

"True faith moves the hand of God."

2 Corinthians 1:20 reads, "For all the promises of God in him are yea and in him amen, unto the glory of God by us." Notice the words "by us." This means we are the ones who have to appropriate the promises. Faith is receiving what He has already done. It's a simple process: God gives us a promise, His promise produces active faith, and then God fulfills the promise.

Faith is a persistent force. Faith never says

"no." Faith knows no defeat. When God says something, faith replies, "Amen. I believe it. That settles it."

"Faith only operates in the realm of the impossible."

James 2:17 says, "In the same way, faith by itself, if it is not accompanied by action, is dead." If faith doesn't have works, or if it's non-productive, it is dead. But have you ever noticed in the Word of God that when things die, they get resurrected? If there's death, there could be a resurrection.

Verse 18 says, "But someone will say, 'You have faith; I have deeds.' Show me your faith without deeds, and I will show you my faith by what I do."

You can't see faith; you can only see what it produces. Faith is a nebulous force. You know

"You know faith by what it produces."

faith by what it produces. If there is nothing to see, it shows that faith is dead and needs to be resurrected.

Verse 20 reads, "You foolish man, do you want evidence that faith without deeds is useless?" Faith produces. So if your faith is alive and well, it will be productive. If your faith does not produce, there is one of two reasons: Either it is dead, or you don't actually know you already have faith.

"Faith that is alive, is also productive."

Chapter Three
THE MEASURE OF FAITH

Romans 12:3 in the Old King James translation says, "To every believer is given the measure of faith.

If you are a believer, the promise in the Word of God is that you have already been given *the* measure of faith.

Upon salvation, Jesus imparts a spirit of faith to us. It comes with the package. You don't have to go out and get faith. God has already imparted a spirit of faith into every believer's life. You are full of faith. You may not feel like it, but you are.

To every believer is given *the* measure of faith. If, in the original translation it said "a" measure, it would mean each of us could potentially receive different amounts. But it says He's given *the* measure. This means there's a particular measurement of faith that God has given us, and every believer was given this measure the day she was saved. It's exactly the same amount of faith imparted to every believer.

"We are given the measure of faith at salvation."

People often say, "Oh, that person has so much more faith than I do." The truth is, the person you regard as a giant of faith received the same original amount of faith as you did. He just knows how to maximise it.

A few years ago, this term "the measure" triggered something in me and I went to the library to study it. I translated it back to its root and from one measurement to another measurement, in order to understand it in today's terms.

The term "the measurement" is an ancient Hebrew weight and measurement and it literally means twelve barrelfuls. In liquid form it is approximately between nine and ten imperial gallons. Each believer, therefore, has twelve barrelfuls of faith living and abiding in him. That's what you start with. You already have enough faith--nine to ten imperial gallons full of it! You are full of faith.

"Each believer receives the same amount of faith."

Enlarging Your Faith Tank

"I tell you the truth, if you have faith as small as a mustard seed, you can say to this mountain, 'Move from here to there' and it will move. Nothing will be impossible for you."
Matthew 17:20 (NIV)

Chapter Four
HOW BIG IS YOUR FAITH?

I used to teach that the mustard seed was the smallest known seed in the world and that we only possess about as much faith as the size of a mustard seed. But when I started reading the Bible for myself and stopped just listening to what others were saying, I discovered that the very first word of Matthew 17:20 is "if."

"If you have faith as a mustard seed, you will say to this mountain, 'Move from here to there,' and it will move; and nothing will be impossible for you." (NKJ)

It's not that your faith is the size of a mustard seed. The Word is saying that even if you only had faith the size of a mustard seed, you would be able to do so much with it. In fact, you'd be able to move mountains!

Imagine then what you could do with twelve barrels full of faith—that's a whole lot of mustard seed! If faith the size of a mustard seed can say to a mountain, "Move!" you'd better be careful what you say in faith, now that you have twelve barrels full!

Chapter Five
FAITH COMES BY HEARING

According to Romans 10 verse 17 faith comes—or is matured, developed and advanced—by hearing. In order to hear the Word of God, it has to be stated. Therefore, don't just think about the Word of God in your mind, or meditate on it in your heart, say it out loud. Faith is developed, matured, advanced and deepened by hearing the Word of God.

"Faith is developed, matured, advanced and deepened by hearing the Word of God."

The apostle Peter says the Word of God is an incorruptible seed, which means the Word never dies; it is eternal. But a seed has to be planted, nurtured and watered in order to produce fruit. For the Word of God to grow and produce fruit in your life, it has to be planted in your spirit. Since seed produces after its own kind (planting pineapples will get you more pineapples) in order to grow the appropriate fruit in your spirit, you need to plant the appropriate Word seed.

If you are experiencing fear, you need to plant seed that will produce power. If you are experiencing sickness, you need to sow God's Word on healing. Sowing the appropriate seed requires knowing what you need.

"Know what you need in order to sow the appropriate seed."

Chapter Six
WHAT DO YOU NEED ME TO DO FOR YOU?

When I have a need, the last thing I do is pray. It doesn't mean that I don't pray, but the last thing I do is pray. Although I can show you one example of a man who didn't believe and still got a miracle, the general rule is that we need to believe when we come to God with our request. The first thing to do is determine what your need is. Yes, God does know what the problem is, but He also wants to know if you know what the true need is. And the Word of God is clear: we get exactly what we ask for.

Matthew 7:7 says, "Ask and it shall be given to you, seek and you shall find, knock and the door shall be opened." The person who asks (and the Greek word here means the person who keeps on asking, keeps on seeking and keeps on knocking) shall receive.

First identify the need. It's not a lack of faith to say what is wrong with you or what you need; it's called honesty. Jesus announced what was wrong with people. He even called the lepers, lepers.

Once you identify what the need is, then go to the Word of God and find out what the Scriptures say. Find the promise of God relevant to your need in His Word.

If you're dealing with sickness, Mark 16:18 says, "Lay hands on the sick and they shall recover." Or Psalm 107:20 says, "He sent his word and healed them all and delivered them from their destruction." In James 5:15 it says, "The prayer of faith shall save the sick."

> **"Faith plants the appropriate seeds."**

Look for the promises relevant to the need. God's Word is an incorruptible seed, and if you plant the right seed in the right soil, you'll get the right fruit.

If your need is finances, pray scriptures like, "Give and it shall be given unto you, pressed down, shaken together and running over." (Luke 6:38) Or, "It is the Lord thy God who giveth thee power to get wealth." (Deuteronomy 8:18)

If you need help, the psalmist David said in Psalm 121:1, "Lift up thine eyes unto the hills from whence cometh thy help, thy help cometh from the Lord."

If you are suffering from depression or oppression, Isaiah 61:3 says "He'll give you the garment of praise for the spirit of heaviness."

If you lack victory? "Nay, in all these things you are more than a conqueror." (Romans 8:37) Or, 2 Corinthians 2: 14 (KJV) "Now thanks be unto God, which always causeth us to triumph in Christ."

If you lack power in your life, look for Acts 1:8. "You shall receive the Holy Ghost and you shall receive power."

If you are bound with some kind of fear, 2 Timothy 1:7 reads, "For God has not given you a spirit of fear, but of power, love and a sound mind."

Go to the Scriptures, and don't just go by what you know and have memorized already. Look for new scriptures that fit your specific need.

Once I have the appropriate verse, I pray and tell God the need. I also pray the answer, which is His Word. I come to Him in prayer and say, "Your

Word says this, this and this. And I've come to receive what Your Word has promised." I simply come to receive the promise of His Word.

Several years ago I needed something from God. I started praying for it a couple of months before I needed it. But three days before the deadline, it still wasn't happening and I was under pressure. It got down to the night before and still nothing was happening. I had to have it by the next morning, so I took my Bible and went outside. I was pretty aggravated because I'd really been praying and even fasted. So I went outside that night and I actually yelled at God: "God, I want you to have a look at something. Come here, have a look!" I pointed at His Word and asked, "Did you or did you not say that?" And since it's His Word and He did say it, I asked, "So where's the answer? For two months I've been believing you and you haven't come through." That's all I did, and I walked inside. It felt pretty good.

The answer came early the next morning. Since I finally got it, you would think I would have been swinging from the chandeliers and shouting with joy. But I wasn't. I went outside that next day and had another little talk with God.

"Now I have a problem," I told Him. "I don't know how to explain this to the people I'll be teaching. How will I explain that you didn't come through until I got angry and yelled at you?"

And God spoke something to me that I've never forgotten. He said, "That had nothing to do with it. That was the first time in two months you came to me on the basis of My Word."

Most Christians come to God on the basis of need. Up until that time, I had been going to Him on the basis of need. I needed to come to Him on the basis of the answer--His Word. Jeremiah 1:12 says that God watches over His word to perform it. When we come to Him on the basis of His Word, by His very nature, God has to see that His Word does what it says. His Word is His will.

"Faith comes to God on the basis of His Word, not the need."

Faith for Daily Use

My son, do not forget my law, [word]
But let your heart keep my commands; [word]
For length of days and long life
And peace they will add to you.
Let not mercy and truth forsake you;
Bind them around your neck,
Write them on the tablet of your heart.
Proverbs 3:1-3 (NKJ)

Chapter Seven
FAITH FROM THE ROCK

Although faith in God started with Abraham, I have learned much about faith from the children of Israel on their journey out of Egypt. God told them to go on a 40-day journey through the wilderness. It turned into a 40-year nightmare. It wasn't God's fault. He gave clear instructions. The Israelites and their leaders didn't believe God.

What's amazing to me is that the Israelites were outside of God's will and yet God kept meeting with them and supplying their needs. He gave them a pillar of fire by night and a pillar of cloud by day. He supplied manna six days a week. To me, this shows the goodness of God's character. Even when we have trouble understanding God, He will not abandon or reject us, but wants to come through for us.

In Exodus 17:1-7 the children of Israel got upset with Moses. They were thirsty and questioned his leadership and authority, even to the point of saying that they would have been better off in Egypt.

When Moses asked God what to do, He said: "Strike the rock, and water will come out of it for the people to drink."

Typology says it's a wonderful picture of Jesus, our Rock, smitten at the cross of Calvary with living water flowing into unbelievers who get right with God.

In Number 20:1-8, we find the same people, the same leadership and the same problems. Full of complaints and criticisms, the Israelites have completely forgotten the miracle God did earlier. Again Moses consulted God and he received a word. Although God's instructions sounded very similar, there were slight differences. God never told Moses to hit the rock; instead He instructed Moses to speak to the rock. In his anger Moses hit it twice. He was disobedient and still, water came out and the people were satisfied. Moses and Aaron, however, paid a price. They could no longer lead the people into Canaan. They did not believe what God had said.

We can learn from their lesson. We received faith when the rock was hit the first time. Once faith is in us, the rock doesn't need to be smitten again; all we have to do is speak to the rock.

Jesus is our Rock. We don't need to smite this Rock; He's already been smitten once and for all. When we avail ourselves of the smitten rock Jesus, He imparts a spirit of faith to us.

Hebrews 12:2 reads, "Looking unto Jesus the author and finisher of our faith." He is the beginning and end of our faith. When we get saved, Jesus puts a spirit of faith in us. He doesn't leave us without faith. He fills us with faith because faith is part of the character of God.

Now we can speak to the Rock. Our Rock is no longer a physical Jesus or a physical rock, but the Word of the Lord. This is His mind, His nature, His being. (I actually believe that if Jesus physically came down here, He'd only tell us what is already in the Word of God.)

Jesus showed us how to get faith, when to get faith and then how to operate in faith.

Chapter Eight
OPERATING IN FAITH

We operate in faith by speaking. The Word of God says, "Faith comes by hearing..." * It is imperative that we don't just read or meditate on it, although these methods are all good. But when we hear the Word of God, our faith is enlarged. No wonder we read many times, "He who has ears to hear, let him hear."

"Faith comes by hearing."

Faith is about relationship. It flows out of our relationship with God.

God wanted Moses to listen to His instruction and not simply act on past experience. In the same way, God wants us to exercise our faith by following His careful instructions, flowing out of our relationship with Him.

When the rock was smitten, He became Jehovah Tsikendu, the Lord our Righteousness. He also became Jehovah Jireh, the Lord will provide. It means we simply have to receive His provision. When Jesus went to the cross, He accomplished everything that needed to be accomplished. Now all we have to do is come and receive what He has done. We already have Jehovah Jireh and His provision shall be seen. It's not "spiritual magic." It's about obeying the right principles.

Chapter Nine
Speaking the Word

Romans 10:8-10 (NKJ) says, "The word is near you, in your mouth and in your heart (that is, the word of faith which we preach): that if you confess with your mouth the Lord Jesus and believe in your heart that God has raised Him from the dead, you will be saved. For with the heart one believes unto righteousness, and with the mouth confession is made unto salvation."

The word is near us. Paul says the word is in our mouth and in our hearts. In verse 10 of Romans 10, however, we find the order has been changed from mouth and heart, to heart and mouth.

Here's what I have learned: The Word has to be in our mouth. When it's in our mouth, we're obviously saying it. Once we're saying it, we hear it and it gets into our heart or our spirit. The only way the Word gets into our heart and our spirit is by revelation. And when it comes out of our heart and spirit onto our lips as confession, it is a confession of the Word of the living God. This is not confession in parrot fashion. It's a revelation of what the Word says, as opposed to what it means.

Confession is about the Word of God. His Word is in your mouth. Not just what the word means, but his Word.

When Kathy and I have a need, the last thing we do is pray. We first establish what the need is. Next we look for God's promises in regards to the need. And then we start saying it, saying it, saying it. I don't believe it's mind over matter. Rather, it's regenerating the mind— getting God's mind into our mind and spirit. I call it "washing" the mind.

God watches over His Word and His promise to perform it. He doesn't watch over what it means or what our need is. He watches over His Word to perform it.

God not only shows us how to get faith, but also how to operate in it. I believe it comes down to saying and hearing. In fact, Psalm 45:1 says, "My tongue is the pen of a ready writer." That is faith in action.

Great Faith
In Luke 7:1-10 we find the story of the centurion whose servant was extremely ill. The servant

suffered from a kind of palsy that made him foam at the mouth and experience intense pain. Because there was no known cure for this illness at the time, the centurion sent some Jewish elders to ask Jesus to come to his home and heal his servant. The centurion, a Roman soldier, commanded the respect of the Jews even though the people in Capernaum were enslaved to the Romans. In fact, the Jewish elders said, "He loves our nation and has built us a synagogue."

While Jesus was on His way to the centurion's home, the centurion sent some of his friends to tell Jesus that He didn't need to come to his house. He said, "But say the word, and my servant will be healed." He then explained his philosophy and understanding of the power of a spoken word by saying, "For I also am a man placed under authority, having soldiers under me. And I say to one, 'Go,' and he goes; and to another, 'Come,' and he comes; and to my servant, 'Do this,' and he does it." He understood the authority in which Jesus operated. He understood that the sickness had to obey the Word of God.

When Jesus heard the centurion's words, He said, "I have not found such great faith, not even in Israel." It probably shocked the disciples to hear Jesus call a Roman soldier, a Gentile, a man of great faith.

Why did this centurion have great faith? He totally believed the word Jesus spoke and he was fully committed to it. He understood the authority of the Word of God. His faith was not necessarily in Jesus' gifts or His ministry, but in Jesus' words.

In John 6:63 (NKJ) Jesus said His words are Spirit and life. But not only are His words full of power and authority, they are also creative. The centurion's friends discovered that the servant was healed at the exact moment Jesus spoke the word.

The Word is God

In John 1:1 we read, "In the beginning was the Word, and the Word was with God, and the Word was God." The reason the Word of God is so powerful, is because the Word is God.

John 1:14 says, "The Word became flesh and dwelt among us." Very simply put, the Word was the physical Jesus. In a sense, today, the Word becomes flesh again every time we apply it. The Word causes needs to dissipate. Sickness leaves, the Word becomes flesh and health appears. Psalm 107:20 says, "He sent His Word and healed them and delivered them from their destructions." It means that as the Word is applied, His Word will heal the sick and deliver His people from all destructive situations.

Seeing Isn't Believing

"Because you have seen me,
you have believed;
blessed are those who have not seen
and yet have believed."
John 20:29 (NIV)

Chapter Ten
LYING SYMPTOMS

In John 20:19-29 the disciples were locked in a room for fear of the Jews. Jesus appeared to them supernaturally and told them that He had been resurrected. They were incredibly excited, seeing Jesus and understanding that He was resurrected. They saw the nail prints in His hands and feet, and the mark in His side from the spear. But Thomas was not with them when it happened. The Bible says Thomas arrived a little later. When they told Him about Jesus' visit and all they had seen Thomas said, "I will not believe unless I see."

Even though we are spiritual entities, very often we act in the realm of the intellect and with a carnal spirit. We say "Unless I see, I will not believe." The truth is that even if we did see, many of us still won't believe. The disciples put up with Thomas for eight days until Jesus appeared again and said to Thomas: "Put your finger here; see my hands. Reach out your hand and put it into my side."
When Thomas finally recognized Him, Jesus said: "Because you have seen me, you have believed; blessed are those who have not seen and

yet have believed." (NIV)

What was He telling Thomas? Perhaps He was saying, "Why didn't you believe what these men told you? They saw me, but you would not believe, O faithless one."

Sometimes we have to struggle for a while, believing that God will come through. Sometimes true faith can be the opposite of sight. Noah had never seen a flood or even heard of one, and yet he believed God, built and ark and survived the flood. We should never go by what we see, or don't see, but rather by the Word of the Living God. Blessed are those who have not seen and yet believe.

Chapter Eleven
JONAH'S STORY

In Jonah we read how Jonah got thrown out of a boat and swallowed by a whale. Bouncing into the belly of the big fish, Jonah repented and started offering sacrifices of thanksgiving and praise to God. In Jonah 2:8 (KJV) he says: "They that observe lying vanities forsake their own mercy." If translated in more modern language, it would sound like this: "They that observe lying symptoms forsake their own deliverance."

I have learned that sickness is a lying symptom. (I didn't say it isn't real.) Being financially broke is another lying symptom. (Again, I didn't say it isn't real.) The Truth, however, is God's Word. Because the Truth is the Word, our symptoms and circumstances are lying symptoms.

Trouble is, symptoms are real. Circumstances and trials are as real as they possibly could be, but God's Word says they're still lying symptoms. And it's the Truth that sets us free.

I had a friend who was blind. He went around saying, "I'm healed, I'm healed." After a while,

I got tired of it and said, "Listen, you're not healed."

He was angry with me for saying that and said, "You just lost my healing for me."

But I said, "I didn't lose you your healing, you never had it to begin with."

Saying "I'm healed" is not confession. Confessing is saying what God's Word says, not what God's Word means. God watches over His Word to perform it.* He doesn't watch over what it means, he watches over His Word.

Chapter Twelve
BELIEVING, NOT SEEING

In Mark 11 verses 12-14 and 20-24 we read about Jesus' encounter with the fig tree. The Bible says Jesus went to get fruit from the fig tree, but found nothing and so He rebuked the fig tree. Approximately 24 hours later, they passed by again and Peter saw a difference in the fig tree. He said to Jesus, "Rabbi, look! The fig tree you cursed has withered!"** Peter was amazed at that.

When Jesus first spoke, it looked like nothing had happened. Peter only saw the difference when they came back the next day. When someone prays, just because we don't see an immediate answer it does not mean that Jesus and His Word are not working. If we go by what we see, we are just like Thomas.

Very often Jesus will start at the root of the problem and work from the inside out. That's what happened with the fig tree: it died at the root and its death only became visible the next day.

I can't tell you how many people we've prayed

for with cancer who didn't get healed immediately, but over night, over a day or over a couple of weeks—whatever the time may be—they were healed. Jesus started His healing work at the root of the problem.

Jesus then turned to Peter and said, "Have faith in God." The Greek literally reads, "Have the faith of God." When we got saved, God put His faith in us. We're not operating on our own faith; we're actually operating on His faith.

I remember the man in Yakima, Washington, who was literally crippled with arthritis. He had to be dressed and bathed. They carried him to the meeting and put him in a lounge chair at the back, because he was in so much pain. When we went to pray for him, it didn't look as if anything had happened. They carried him home that night and laid him in bed. At 2 a.m., the bed shook and threw him out of the bed and onto the floor. He got up and got back into bed. A few minutes later it shook again. It threw him out of the bed and onto the floor. He got off the floor and back into bed and mumbled, "I can't believe these earthquakes." Finally, when it happened the third time, the man got up and realized that all three times he was doing something he couldn't do before.

It wasn't a normal earthquake, but a Holy Spirit earthquake by the power of Almighty God.

We shouldn't observe the lying symptoms. Our eyes should be focused on the living God and His Word.

Galatians 2 verse 20 says: "I have been crucified with Christ; it is no longer I who live, but Christ lives in me; and the life which I now live in the flesh I live by faith in the Son of God, who loved me and gave Himself for me."

We are living by God's faith. In Habakkuk 2 verse 4 it also says that we live by the faith of the Son of God. When you live by His faith, there's no fight, there's no struggle. When you rest in the Word of God and His anointing, it is God who does the work.

When we were pastoring, early on in our ministry, Kathy told me she was believing for a sizeable sum of money. Several days later she came to me and said she had the money. I wanted to see it and even touch it. (We didn't have much in those days). But she said 'no.' I kept asking and she kept saying 'no.' The next day when the mail arrived, there was a letter for Kathy. Inside was a check made out for the exact amount she had believed for.

When I saw her with the check, I thought she had double because the day before she told me she already had the money. I said, "Wow! Now you have double." And she said, "No, this is what I had yesterday. Yesterday I knew God had done it. This came today because yesterday I knew I had it. No one told me they were sending it to me; I just knew God had heard my prayer and the answer was on the way."

In a similar way, Joshua believed God when He said He would give him Jericho. Even when God said march around the city, instead of warring for it. Imagine Joshua trying to convince his generals that this was how they would defeat Jericho. But Joshua believed God's Word – they marched and indeed the walls came down.

Chapter Thirteen
WAR OF THE SENSES

Most of us are governed by our five senses: sight, sound, touch, taste and smell. How many times does it happen that if we can't see something, we believe it doesn't exist. Or if we can't feel it, it hasn't happened. The five natural senses only sense what they know, but faith knows what is True, regardless of what the senses indicate.

In 2 Corinthians 5:7, The Bible says, "We walk by faith and not by sight." As believers, we have been given a spirit of faith and it is faith that should govern and dictate our spiritual life.

The senses constantly war against the spirit, however. They will tell us it's not God. Or that it's not right. The senses will tell us it's not going to happen. But when we operate in faith, we don't go by our senses. We go by the Word of the living God because it is inspired of God, filled with God and it is the mind of God.

We've been taught that our senses will tell us what's going on. But the truth is, they don't. God told Abraham three times that he was going to have a son. On one occasion, God took

Abram outside, showed him the stars and said, "So shall your offspring be." ***

Abraham never talked about it. Instead, with the help of Sarah, they tried to manipulate the Word of God. Abraham got involved with Hagar who then gave birth to Ishmael.

Ironically, Abraham used to say, "Seeing you've given me no heir, is the one in my house my heir?" Abraham was referring to Eleazer, the chief of all the slaves, although he knew very well that Eleazer wasn't what the Lord meant by an heir. Abraham, however, depended on what he could see. "Seeing you have given me no heir."

Still, Abraham became the father of faith. In Romans 4 verses 17-24 we read an account of this faith.

Abraham knew God was well able to do it, even though it was impossible in the natural realm. And God did it by assuring Abraham that He knew him. It was a biological impossibility, but God came through.

Remember when we talked about "you've got to say it to hear it?" Abraham never talked about what God was going to do. So God got Abraham to say it by changing his name from Abram to Abraham. That meant every time someone went up to Abraham and said his name, Abraham heard "father of many nations." Even Sarah got to hear it whenever she said her husband's name: Abraham, father of many nations.

Although faith comes by hearing, the Bible also says faith that without works is dead. There had to be some action in the tent. There had to be faith with works.

Hebrews 11:11 says, "By faith Sarah herself also received strength to conceive seed, and she bore a child when she was past the age, because she judged Him faithful who had promised." Sarah was hearing it too.

Chapter Fourteen
IN THE BEGINNING

In Genesis chapter one, every time God declared something into being, the Bible said it happened. Even God had to have faith in His own word. He didn't go out into the cosmos and have a trial run to see if it would work. He came in and he spoke it and every time he spoke it, it came into being. That principle has not changed. That's how it began and His word does not alter. God's word is real and powerful. It has an integrity that is beyond reproach.

In fact, Genesis 1 verse 3 says, "And God said let there by light and there was light." In the Hebrew, if we translated it literally into English, it reads, "God said light be and light was."

So powerful is God's Word that when God spoke and said, "Light be," He had to immediately put it in the past tense and say, "Light was." That's the Word that brings faith to us. That's the Word that develops, matures, advances and increases our faith. For faith comes by hearing the Word of God.

According to Hebrews 13:8 says Jesus Christ is

the same yesterday, today and forever. If He's the same, then His Word is the same. "I am the Lord and I change not." He is by name what He is by nature and He is by demonstration what He is by declaration.

Over 2,000 times in the Word of God we read, "God says" or "thus saith the Lord" and every time God said these, they came into being. God created the earth and introduced man to earth by the words of His mouth. He married spiritual words with a physical world. He released His faith within His Word. And He still does.

Hebrews 11 verse 3 says, "By faith we understand that the worlds were framed by the word of God, so that the things which are seen were not made of things which are visible." The apparent, spiritual substance to everything that we touch, taste, smell, feel and see is the faith of God in the Word of God. The Word of God will not fail. It will not cease and it will not die. Psalm 119:89 says, "Forever, O LORD, Your word is settled in heaven."

Numbers 23:19 says, "God is not a man, that He should lie, nor a son of man, that He should repent. Has He said, and will He not do? Or has He spoken, and will He not make it good?" What

God's Word says, God's Word will do. It's up to us to believe it and experience the blessings that come with faith.

Jeremiah 1:12
Mark 11:21
*** *Genesis 15:5*

Developing Your Personal Faith

*"When Jesus saw their faith,
he said to the paralytic,
'Son, your sins are forgiven.'"
Mark 2:5 (NIV)*

Chapter Fifteen
ELIJAH'S STORY

In I Kings 17 and 18 we read some of the highlights of the prophet Elijah's supernatural ministry. The scriptures have keys, principles and guidance for us and this part of Elijah's ministry is no exception. It really gives us insight into a personal walk of faith.

In I Kings 17:1-7, Elijah has prophesied to King Ahab that there would be no rain for several years. God then tells him to go and hide at the brook Cherith and drink water from the brook. He commanded ravens to feed him and they brought Elijah bread and meat every morning and evening. What was happening here? I believe God was beginning to develop Elijah's ministry. The key is that Elijah has to accept it, walk in it, and live in it.

Living by faith is a lifestyle. It is not just having faith for certain things or times. It is living in faith and by faith 24 hours a day; not going from calamity to calamity. God's supply and provision is ongoing, continuous, never ceasing. He is the God who supplies, not simply the God who supplies "on occasion." "God provides all of your need (note it is singular nor plural), according to His riches and glory." God sees everything we have need of as one continual need.

Elijah found himself developing his personal faith. We are not going to minister to the needs of others or take a city for God until we learn to believe God for ourselves. The situation he now found himself in was not easy. In fact, I imagine it was quite difficult. Ravens bringing food sounds simple. But the word "ravens" in the original Hebrew means "dirty birds." I am told it is quite possible the food they brought could have been contaminated. Elijah had to believe God for the food to be edible.

The prophecy to Ahab came to pass and the ravens did supply food every day. Even though the situation was difficult, Elijah survived and saw a miracle of provision. You and I need to believe God for ourselves – soon it will become a lifestyle.

After this God spoke to Elijah again, to go to Zarapheth and there a widow would provide for him (I Kings 17:8-16). Actually, it was not what this widow woman was going to do for Elijah but what Elijah was going to do for her. He had passed the first test for himself so now he could minister to someone else. He proved God personally and privately, and now was branching out beyond himself. He was seeing God miraculously and supernaturally provide for others.

At this point Elijah has nowhere to live and nothing to eat. I'm sure he was thinking her to be a rich widow, someone who had the means to take care of his needs. I mean if God said she would be able to provide for him – she would have the ability! Little did he know that he was going to have to minister to her need. For in reality, she had so little it was really quite pitiful!

There was a war at that time and there were many widows in Zarapheth (the men had died during this war). Elijah's first clue that the widow didn't have much was that she was picking up sticks near the gate of the city in order to make a fire and cook. If she were rich, a maid would have been doing it for her. Can you imagine how Elijah felt? What he was thinking? Thank God, faith is not determined by how we feel or what we think. Now he approaches her and asks for some water. As she is going to get water he says to her, "Please also give me some bread." This is not much to ask for, a simple request. But now he is about to enter an entirely different arena. What was impossible to the widow, God would make possible through Eljah's obedience. Elijah has now progressed to the realm of ministering to someone beyond himself - learning to release faith.

Elijah had successfully been able to believe God for himself and see the supernatural provision. Now he is believing for a woman with a gigantic need. This woman responds to Elijah, "I do not have any bread, only a handful of flour in a bin, and a little oil. I am gathering a couple of sticks that I may prepare to cook the last meal for my son and myself. Then we will eat it, lay down and die. This is all we have and it is our last meal. We cannot survive."

In the natural it seemed hopeless for both Elijah and the widow. It is possible that she did not want to give Elijah her last meal and he is thinking he should not take it. Who would have blamed him? Elijah moves out of the natural into the spiritual, into the realm of faith. Any need that we have is really an opportunity for God to work a miracle. The need is not an obstacle but a glorious opportunity for a miracle. I encourage you to get ready for God's provision and miracles through you to others.

Chapter Sixteen
STEPS TO A MIRACLE POSITION

Elijah says there are five steps for this lady to take. (1 Kings 17:13 and 14)

1. **"Do not fear."** That is the direct command from the man of God. Fear is the opposite of faith, yet almost the same principle as faith. Fear is believing the miracle won't or cannot happen. Fear does not come from God. 2 Timothy 1:7 says, "For God has not given us a spirit of fear, but a spirit of power and of love and of a sound mind." Fear drives the miracle away, faith brings the miracle to you.

2. **"Go and do as you have said."** Get on with what you planned, don't sit and wait. Some people never receive because they never do anything. I was ministering on finances and the principle that if you won't work, the Bible says you shouldn't eat. I'm not saying, if you cannot work. One man shouted to me that he had been unemployed for several years and there were no jobs available. This was very real to this man and others in the church. I responded, "I believe you but God

is bigger than that and can open up employment for you in spite of the economic problems." I challenged him and others to meet me at the church the next morning. Together we knocked on the doors of businesses and asked for employment. By noon all three had several job opportunities and by the next day, all three were employed! We were actually able to give the extra employment opportunities to others in the church. We had to "go" and "do" something.

3. **"Make me a small cake."** God will take what you have and multiply it. Use what you have so God can give you what you do not have. One of the things I have learned: do not hold onto even the very last that you have. Use it now. Don't be foolish, but use it wisely and watch God do a miracle!

4. **"Bring it to me."** Elijah is now getting her to give - teaching her to sow something. In her hour of need she is being taught Godly principles about sowing and reaping. He is saying to her, "I am not going to get it. You bring it and give it to me." Luke 6:39 says, "Give and it shall be given unto you, good measure, pressed down, running over, will be put in your bosom, for with the same mea-

sure that you use, it shall be measured back to you." I know this scripture is primarily about forgiveness, but this Godly principle works in many aspects of life and God.

5. **"...And afterwards make some for yourself and your son."** Wait a minute! She only had enough for one last meal. The prophet Elijah has taken what was left for the widow and her son. How in the world could she make another meal? Naturally, we would ask the same questions. We have God's word and yet we are not sure if God can do the miraculous. We ask questions. What if it does not happen? What if it does not come to pass? Well, what if it does? God is an awesome God! Nothing is too hard for God. Nothing is impossible with God. He can and will do it for you. Don't give up, hold on.

Elijah is positioning her for the miracle she needs. Notice that the widow has not said anything about receiving. Elijah just nudges her a little here, a little there, until she is positioned to receive. Sometimes Pastors and leaders need to learn how to get people positioned to receive. There are times when people I have ministered to are not aware that I am helping position them to receive.

Remember in Mark 2:1-12, Jesus is preaching in a house that is packed with people. A paralyzed man is carried to the house by four friends. They cannot get him to Jesus because of the crowds, but they don't give up. The men cut a hole in the roof and lowered their sick friend into the room where Jesus was ministering. They didn't give up and do nothing. They put action to their belief. They were determined to get the friend positioned so he could receive his miracle. It was more about their faith than his. Verse five says, "Jesus saw their faith." In Luke 5:17-26 we have the same story. Notice verse 17, "The power of the Lord was present to heal." Only one man was healed – no one else – none of the religious people. They were there to observe, question, resist, rebuke and argue. The paralyzed man's friends positioned him and he received his miracle.

Elijah now speaks a clear, direct and prophetic word in verse 14-16. "For thus, says the Lord God of Israel, the bin of flour shall not be used up, nor shall the jar of oil run dry until the day the Lord sends rain upon the earth. So they went away and did according to the words of Elijah and he and her household ate for many days. The bin of flour was not used up, nor did the jar of oil run dry." Not only did Elijah's needs get taken care of, but the woman and her son entered into an ongoing miracle of provision. Now he is ready to take on bigger things.

Things

In I Kings 18:20-46, Elijah is now ready to take on 450 men, the Prophets of Baal, and he is alone. He challenges the people in verse 21, "How long will you falter between two opinions?" This man is now strong in faith ready to subdue nations and false prophets. He is full of active faith. He issues an incredible challenge, each side to build an altar and whoever's God consumes it with fire will be the proof. That is the one and true real God - the other is false religion. The nation is watching. Verse 20 says "all" the children of Israel had been sent for to gather at Mt. Carmel. Bulls were killed and put on the altars along with wood and the 450 prophets called on Baal to consume their offering with fire, to prove he was the true God. From early morning to early evening they called, shouted, jumped, cut themselves with knives until blood gushed out of them and no answer from Baal. Elijah mocked them, "Maybe your god is meditating, or busy, or has gone on a journey, or perhaps he is sleeping." (Verse 27)

Now it becomes Elijah's turn. He repairs the altar of the Lord, (verse 30) then he built an altar in the name of the Lord. When we move in faith, we do it in the name of the Lord not in our own strength. He then built a trench around it (verse 32) large enough to hold two seahs of seed. He told the people to fill the water pots with water and pour it on the burnt sacrifice and wood (verse 33). They were to do that three times and fill the trench with water. Elijah called on God to consume the altar and water with fire and let the people know He was the true God. Verse 38, "Then the fire of the Lord fell and consumed the burnt sacrifice and the wood and the stones and the dust and it licked up the water that was in the trench." Verse 39 "...Now when all the people saw it they fell on their faces and said, 'the Lord, he is God.'" All of the prophets of Baal were executed.

Chapter Seventeen
NOTHING IS TOO HARD FOR GOD

Notice what Elijah did. He made the miracle provision as difficult for God as he could. We try to make it easy for God, but "nothing is too hard for the Lord." There are 10 things Elijah did at Mt. Carmel.

1. He called the people to observe.
2. He challenged the people to make a choice – a decision.
3. He declared he was the true man of God (prophet).
4. He recognized one man with God is a majority.
5. He wasn't intimidated by the crowd or the thinking of these false prophets. (Don't be intimidated by the circumstances of what's going on around you.)
6. He challenged their belief system.
7. He put God to the test and God came through.
8. He increased the circumstances to make it a bigger and greater miracle.
9. He did it in the name of the Lord.
10. He destroyed the false prophets.

Where did he learn how to move in faith in this magnitude? When he was at the brook Cherith believing God for his daily provision, and when he ministered to the needs of the widow of Zaraphath. These were the steps to fulfilling his public ministry and keys he learned in private ministry.

Life is a journey. We develop our faith God has given us on this journey so that in time we can speak to mountains (not just hills) and they shall obey us and move.

You are full of faith! Nothing is impossible because of the supernatural ability in you.